ARENA
POCKET
GUIDE

BEGINNING
English
Exercises

CHERRY HILL

D1506677

Storey Publishing

*The mission of Storey Publishing is to serve our customers by
publishing practical information that encourages personal
independence in harmony with the environment.*

Edited by Deborah Burns and Aimee Poirier
Cover design by Eugenie Delaney
Front cover photograph by Cherry Hill, back cover
 photograph by Richard Klimesh
Text design by Cindy McFarland
Production assistance by Susan Bernier
Line drawings designed by Cherry Hill and drawn by
 Peggy Judy

   The information in this book is true and complete to the best of our
knowledge. All recommendations are made without guarantee on the part
of the author or Storey Publishing. The author and publisher disclaim any
liability in connection with the use of this information. For additional
information please contact Storey Publishing, 210 MASS MoCA Way,
North Adams, MA 01247.

   Storey books are available for special premium and promotional uses
and for customized editions. For further information, please call 1-800-
793-9396.

Printed in Canada by Transcontinental Printing
10 9 8 7

Library of Congress Cataloging-in-Publication Data

Hill, Cherry, 1947–
   Beginning English exercises / Cherry Hill.
      p.   cm. — (Arena pocket guide)
   ISBN 1-58017-044-7 (pbk. : alk. paper)
   1. Horsemanship. 2. Horses — Training. I. Title. II. Series:
Hill, Cherry, 1947– Arena pocket guide.
SF309.H632 1998
798.2'3—dc21   97-49043
                                                                    CIP

Beginning English Exercises

Arena exercises are a cross between gymnastics, meditation, and geometry. They are essential keys for discovering many important principles about training and riding.

Goals
- Develop rider balance
- Find a steady rhythm
- Establish energetic forward movement
- Maintain left to right balance; ride straight
- Learn the gaits
    Walk
    Posting trot
    Sitting trot
    Canter
- Learn transitions
    Walk to halt, halt to walk
    Walk to trot, trot to walk
    Trot to canter, canter to trot
- Begin bending work
    Riding a corner
    Change of rein on the diagonal

Remember as you practice that it is the QUALITY of the work that is most important. It is a much greater accomplishment to do simple things well than it is to stumble through advanced maneuvers in poor form and with erratic rhythm. Keep your mind in the middle and a leg on each side.

How Can You Tell If the Work Is Correct?

1. Work regularly with a qualified instructor.

2. Ask a qualified person to stand on the ground, observe your exercises, and report to you what he or she sees.

3. Have someone record your exercises on videotape. Then watch the tape carefully using slow motion and freeze frame.

4. As you ride, watch yourself and your horse in large mirrors on the wall.

5. Without moving your head, glance down at your horse's shoulders, neck, poll, and eye during different maneuvers to determine if he is correct up front.

6. Ultimately, the key is to develop a *feel* for when things are going right and when they are going wrong by utilizing all of the above feedback techniques. Answer the following by feeling, not looking:

* Is there appropriate left to right balance on my seat bones? Can I feel them both?
* Can I feel even contact on both reins?
* Is the front to rear balance acceptable or is the horse heavy on the forehand, croup up, back hollow?
* Is the rhythm regular or does the horse speed up, slow down, or break gait?
* Is my horse relaxed or is his back tense?
* Is he on the bit or above or behind it?
* Am I posting on the correct diagonal?
* Is my horse cantering on the correct lead?
* Can I tell when his inside hind leg is about to land?

What Do You Do When Things Go Wrong?

1. Review each component of an exercise.

2. You may need to return to some very basic exercises to establish forward movement, acceptance of contact, or response to sideways driving aids. Returning to simple circle work will often improve straightness and subsequently improve lateral work and collection.

3. Ride an exercise that the horse does very well, such as the walk-trot-walk transition. Work on purity and form.

4. Perform a simpler version of the exercise. If it is a canter exercise, try it at a walk or trot first.

5. Perform the exercise in the opposite direction. Sometimes, because of an inherent stiffness or crookedness in a horse, you will have difficulty with an exercise to the left but no problems to the right! Capitalize on this by refining your skills and the application of your aids in the "good" direction and then return to the "hard" direction with a renewed sense of what needs to be done. I often find that doing work to the right improves work to the left.

At the Halt

How to Evaluate Your Position at the Halt

Note: In each question, the desirable is mentioned first.

* Is your breathing deep and regular, or are you holding your breath?
* Is there equal weight on both seat bones, or is it difficult to feel one of them? Are your seat bones in the deepest part of the saddle, or are you braced against the cantle?
* Are your hip bones directly over your seat bones, or are they behind your seat bones in the "Cadillac" position?
* Is your lower back relaxed, or is it braced and tense?
* Is your upper body above your hips, or is it leaning extremely forward or backward?
* Is there a straight line from your shoulder through your hip to your heel, or are your legs way in front of your body? Are you slumped forward, or are you leaning back?
* Are your shoulders back, or are they rounded forward?
* Is your sternum lifted upward, or is it collapsed inward?
* Are your shoulders level, or is one higher than the other?
* Are your head and neck straight, or are they tilted to one side or rolling forward?
* Are your eyes looking straight ahead, or are they looking down?
* Are your thighs relaxed, or are they gripping or forcibly stretching?
* Do you have appropriate lower leg contact, or are you holding your lower legs away from your horse?

* Can you see just the toe of your boot when you glance down at your foot, or is most of your foot and part of your lower leg visible?
* Is there equal weight in each of your stirrups?
* Are your hands at an even, appropriate level? Is there a direct line from the bit to your elbows?
* Is there even contact on the reins?
* If your horse suddenly disappeared out from under you, would you topple over when you landed on the ground, or would you stand?

The halt should be square and balanced with the horse's legs under his body. The halt is a perfect time to check your position before you begin moving your horse.

If your horse halts square, he will tend to move forward in balance.

The halt is necessary for training-level dressage and all English competitions.

Working Walk

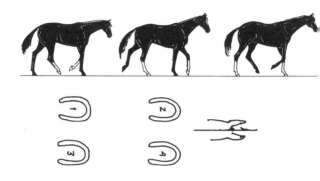

The walk is a four-beat gait that should have a clear, even rhythm as the feet land and take off in the following sequence: left hind, left front, right hind, right front. The walk has alternating lateral and triangular bases of support. At one moment, the horse's weight is borne by two left legs, then the right hind is added, forming a triangle of support. Later in the cycle, all weight is borne by two right legs. That's why the walk creates a side-to-side and front-to-back motion in the saddle. A dressage horse should walk with head and neck unconstrained and lightly on the bit. The speed of the average walk is about 4 miles per hour. The hind footprints should at least touch or land partially on top of the front prints, but ideally the hind prints should be in front of the imprints of the forefeet.

To get in tune with a horse's normal walk:

- Sit with a relaxed seat and legs.
- Let your body sway to the horse's movement.
- Note that at one moment your right leg will swing against the horse's barrel and your left leg will swing away from it. In the next instant, the opposite will occur.

A horse that is rushing at the walk might either jig or prance — impure gaits composed of half walking, half trotting. He might also develop a pacey walk. The pace is a two-beat lateral gait in which the two right limbs rise and land alternately with the two left limbs. Although the pace is a natural gait for some Standardbred horses and other breeds, a pacey walk is considered an impure gait for most riding horses because the even four-beat pattern of the walk has been broken and the walk becomes almost a two-beat gait. This is a difficult habit to change and so must be prevented.

A horse that is walking too slowly often lacks the energy (impulsion) to properly flex his joints. As a result, he drags his toes and might stumble.

A walk can easily be spoiled by bad riding.
Signs of a good walk:

★ a relaxed back
★ a raised and swinging tail
★ a slight head nod and swing, side to side as well as up and down

---

The working walk is used in training-level dressage and all English performances.

Working Trot (Posting Trot)

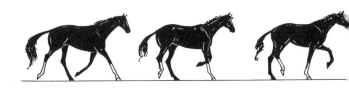

- Rise and sit with the corresponding movement of the horse's outside diagonal (inside hind leg and outside foreleg). *Inside* customarily refers to the inside of a circle or turn, which is often also the inside of the arena. *Outside* refers to the side of the horse nearest the arena rail. When tracking to the left in an arena, the outside diagonal is the right diagonal.
- As the horse's left hind and right front legs are landing underneath you and accepting weight, you should be sitting. As those legs push off and are in the air (swinging forward), you should be rising.
- Learn to feel the action of the inside hind leg by having a ground person tell you each time it has landed.
- If you must work alone, you can check to see if you are on the correct diagonal by carefully glancing down at the horse's outside shoulder. When the outside shoulder is farthest forward, you should be at the peak of your rising.
- Never lean over to check if you are on the correct diagonal. Use only your eyes, because even a simple tilt of the head can throw your body off balance.
- When rising, balance over the center of your foot. Do not allow your foot to swing backward or forward as you rise, which will greatly reduce your stability.

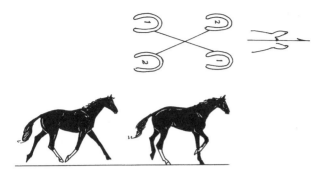

- Rise using your thigh muscles and pivot at your knees. Be careful not to grip with your knees. Although your weight should be deep in your heels during posting, you should not post by pushing yourself up from your stirrups.
- When you sit, land in the saddle softly.
- If you find you are on the incorrect diagonal, simply sit two beats and resume your normal posting rhythm.
- You should be able to post without stirrups.

Description

The trot is a two-beat diagonal gait in which the right front and left hind legs (called the right diagonal) rise and fall together and the left front and right hind legs (called the left diagonal) rise and fall together. Between the landings of the diagonal pairs, there is a moment of suspension that results in a springy gait. The working trot is an active, ground-covering trot. Posting allows you to ride an actively trotting horse more smoothly, and the horse can support a rider's weight better in turns if the rider sits with the inside hind. The average speed of a working trot is 6–8 miles per hour. The hind feet should step into the tracks of the front feet.

The working trot is used in training-level dressage and hunter under saddle.

Sitting Trot

- Regulate your breathing.
- Position your seat bones so they are directly underneath you, not rolled in front of you or squashed out behind you.
- Check to see that your upper body is directly over your seat bones and that your shoulders are over your hips.
- Keep your lower back straight, not hollow, and support it with muscle strength from your abdominal muscles.
- Periodically open your thighs so that they fall vertically along the horse's sides and let your seat bones drop even more deeply on the saddle.
- Lightly embrace your horse's ribs with your lower legs.

Description

Trot refers to the gait as performed under English tack with a marked length of stride and good impulsion.

Since the sitting trot is usually the most steady, stable, and rhythmic of a horse's gaits, it is useful for developing the rider's seat. It is also the cornerstone of many exercises for the horse's training.

* Do not grip with your thighs or knees because the resulting tension will lift you right out of the saddle.
* Don't be tempted to lean your upper body backward at an extreme angle because this will roll your seat bones too far forward and cause your legs to swing out ahead of you, causing you to lose stability.
* When first learning to sit the trot, avoid developing tension and over-riding with the bridle. Otherwise, the horse may develop a hollow back and high head.
* When trotting, take care not to go too slow or the horse's gait might become impure when the diagonal pairs of legs "break" and no longer land and take off at the same time. When the foreleg lands before its diagonal hind leg, the horse has lost suspension entirely and is walking in front and trotting behind.

The sitting trot is required in training-level dressage and most other English performances.

Working Canter

Keep your horse on the correct lead. Ride every step to keep him in balance and in the correct position.

How to Ride the Canter, Right Lead

- Keep your right seat bone forward and your left seat bone in normal position.
- Hold your upper body erect.
- Hold your shoulders even unless you are turning.
- Keep your right leg on the girth, actively, creating right bend and keeping the horse up on left rein.
- Keep your left leg behind the girth, actively, maintaining impulsion and keeping the horse's hindquarters from swinging to the left.
- Apply right direct rein to create the appropriate amount of bend and flexion.
- Maintain left supporting rein.

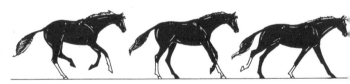

A = *canter left lead*

B = *canter right lead*

Description of Footfall Pattern

1. Initiating hind leg (outside hind)
2. Diagonal pair (inside hind and outside foreleg)
3. Leading foreleg (inside foreleg)
4. Regrouping of legs (a moment of suspension)

If the initiating hind leg is the left, the diagonal pair will consist of the right hind and the left front. The leading foreleg will be the right front and the horse will be on the right lead. When observing a horse on the right lead from the side, his right legs will reach farther forward than his left legs. The right hind will reach under his belly farther than the left hind; the right front will reach out in front of his body farther than the left front. When turning to the right, the horse should be on the right lead.

In a canter, the energy rolls from rear to front, then during a moment of suspension the horse gathers his legs up to get organized for the next set of leg movements. The rider seems to glide until the initiating hind lands and begins the cycle again.

The working canter is used in all English performances and training-level dressage.

Corner

Riding the correct normal corner to the right:

- Trot.
- When you are 20 feet from the rail, increase rein contact momentarily.
- Transfer your weight to your inside seat bone (right) and forward.
- Deepen your right knee (heel down) to prevent your right side from collapsing.
- Flex the horse to the inside with the inside (right) rein.
- Use the inside (right) leg at the girth to cause the horse's inside (right) hind to reach forward and give the horse's body a point to bend around.
- Let the outside (left) rein yield enough to allow the flexion required.
- Maintain enough contact with the outside (left) rein to keep the horse from bulging his outside (left) shoulder to the left.
- Use the outside (left) leg slightly behind the girth to prevent the hindquarters from stepping to the left.
- Use the outside (left) leg to bend the horse around your inside (right) leg.

A deep corner is a more advanced maneuver ridden in collected gaits.

- ★ Keep your inside hand from crossing the mane or you will cause the left shoulder to bulge outward.
- ★ Be sure to maintain the same rhythm through the corner.

If a horse tries to cut the corner with no lateral bend, you must react instantly and decisively with a strong inside leg, seat, and rein.

Arena key from starting dot:

- ★ Correct normal corner for working gaits
- ★ Cutting the corner, flat with no lateral bend
- ★ Incorrect deep corner with too much neck bend from too strong an inside rein
- ★ Correct deep corner for collected gaits

Straight

- Check your own straightness.
- Working trot, sitting.
- Corner.
- Straighten by bringing the forehand in front of the hindquarters. When tracking right, if the horse is counter-flexed left and the right hind is inside the track:
  - Place right leg behind the girth to prevent any more sideways deviation of right hind leg.
  - Right rein in a lifting motion to bring right front shoulder in front of right hind leg.
  - Keep left leg at the girth to keep the left hind moving forward.
  - Keep left rein low and supporting.
- Ride the corner.
- Ride straight about 20–40 feet.
- Turn down the centerline.
- Ride straight without use of arena wall or rail.

Most horses (80–90 percent) travel crooked because the left side is stronger than the right side.

When going to the left, the horse overbends to the left, weights the left shoulder, and swings the hindquarters off the track to the right.

When going to the right, the horse's neck almost counter-flexes to the left (counter-bends with a straight stiffness), and the hindquarters swing to the right.

About 10–20 percent of horses travel crooked in the opposite way.

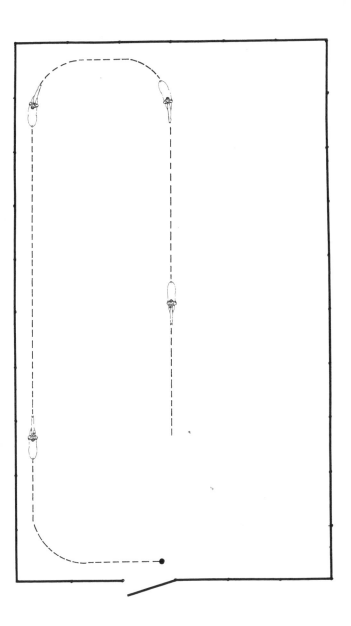

Change of Rein on Long Diagonal

- Posting trot to the left, sitting when the right front and left hind legs land, and rising when they rise.
- Ride the short end.
- Ride the second corner of the short end with a normal left corner.
- After the corner, ride straight 1–2 strides.
- Turn left and head diagonally across the arena, aiming at a point on the opposite long side about two strides from the opposite corner.
- Somewhere in the vicinity of the middle of the diagonal line, change the diagonal to which you are posting by sitting two beats instead of one. This will put you on the new diagonal.
- As you approach the corner, change to right bend.
- Turn right at the end of the diagonal.
- Ride straight 1–2 strides.
- Ride a right corner, and proceed in new direction.

The change of rein on a long diagonal is a roomy way to change direction and bend. You have plenty of time to get organized for changing your seat, leg, and rein aids for the new bend. Properly executed, the rhythm and frame of the horse are consistent throughout the exercise.

★ If your horse throws his head up, rushes forward, shortens his stride, or bobs his head down during the change, improve the coordination of your aids.
★ Be careful not to pull back on the reins when you change your posting because this will cause your horse to lose his balance or shorten his stride.
★ Do not make a diagonal directly from one corner to another because you will have to make very sharp

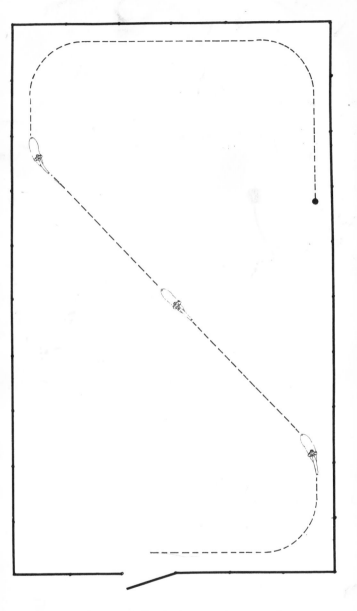

turns that will be difficult for your horse to do without interrupting his balance and rhythm.

★ Do not try to change rein on a diagonal from the *first* corner of the short side because this will force you to make very sharp turns.

Walk—Posting Trot—Walk

- Walk.
- Walk the corner.
- When horse is straight, apply aids for sitting trot.
- Sitting trot 2 strides.
- Post 4 strides.
- Sitting trot 2 strides.
- Walk.
- Walk 1½ strides.
- Sitting trot 2 strides.
- Posting trot 4 strides.
- Sitting trot 2 strides.
- Walk 1½ strides.
- Sitting trot 2 strides.
- Posting trot 4 strides.
- Corner at posting trot.
- When horse is straight, ride the sitting trot 2 strides.
- Walk.
- Halt.
- Perform exercise in opposite direction.

At first, just do one set of transitions on a long side, and gradually work up to two sets.

With each downward transition, the horse collects more. You should be able to feel him sitting down more behind and coming into your hand. His neck and poll should rise.

With each upward transition, you should feel the horse's springiness increase, and as a result he should begin lifting his back with a slight arch.

This exercise gives you a chance to work on the timing of the application of your aids.

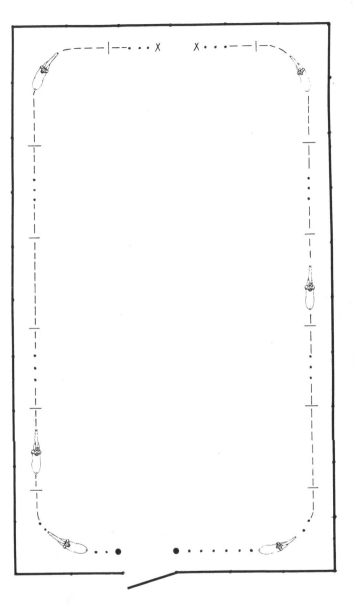

If you do not have a solid, sensitive, following seat at the trot, the few strides of sitting trot in this exercise may cause discomfort to your horse's back. He may hollow his back and perform rough transitions. Perfect your work at a posting trot before trying any sitting trot exercises.

Trot — Canter — Trot

- At **A,** working trot in a large circle to the right.
- At **A,** canter right lead:
  - Momentarily increase light contact on the reins.
  - Right leg at the girth causing horse's right hind to reach farther forward, creating right bend and keeping horse up on left rein.
  - Add more with right rein to produce right flexion at poll.
  - Maintain left rein contact to control right flexion and limit the reach of the left foreleg.
  - Left leg behind the girth to control the hindquarters and prevent the left hind from stepping to the left.
  - Push right seat bone forward with weight in right stirrup (lower your knee and heel) to keep from collapsing your right side while weighting your right seat bone.
  - Apply pressure with both legs: right at the girth and left behind the girth.
  - Apply forward pressure with both seat bones, rolling forward from the left to the right, but don't lean forward or you'll lose your left seat bone. And don't pump your upper body as this tends to hollow the horse's back.
  - Follow canter movement with a vertical upper body and inside (right) hip forward.
  - Don't let your left shoulder fall behind and don't let your outside leg come off the horse.
- At **A,** trot large circle:
  - Move left leg to girth.
  - Maintain a still seat and flex abdominals.
  - Re-balance seat slightly to outside.
  - Close hands on reins, slightly more on left.
- As soon as horse trots, yield with both hands to re-establish softness.
- Change seat to a following trot seat.

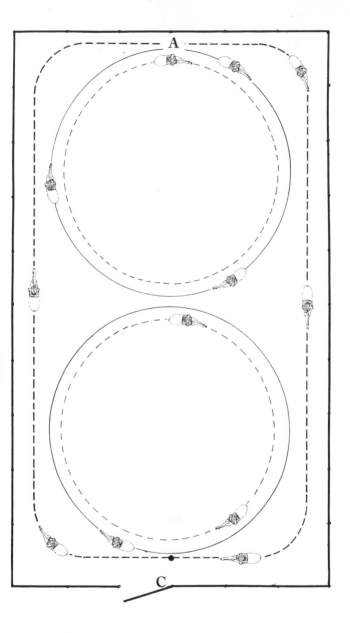

- Open and close hands on reins for a few consecutive strides to regain desired rhythm and balance.
- Trot arena at large from **A** to **C** and repeat exercise.
- Reverse and ride in the opposite direction.

Preparing for Your Test

Work regularly with a qualified instructor.

Practice all the exercises in this guide in both directions.

Visualize the test pattern, "ride" it in your mind. Draw the pattern on a piece of paper several times to be sure you know the order of maneuvers.

Practice individual portions of the test with your horse, but don't over-practice the actual pattern or your horse will anticipate. Anticipation leads to rushed work and errors.

Choose your examiner carefully. You may wish to use your regular instructor or another experienced rider, trainer, or instructor. If you ask someone inexperienced to evaluate you, you'll get unproductive results.

Make photocopies of the score sheet. Since you may want to ride the test several times, have extra copies of the score sheet available.

Arrange to have your test videotaped. Later you can compare the examiner's notes with your actual ride.

Rider warm-up. This is accomplished both in and out of the saddle.

Loosen up by giving your horse a vigorous grooming.

Test your suppleness as you squat down to put on your horse's boots. If you are stiff, do some stretches before you mount up.

Once mounted, do a few upper body stretches, arm circles, leg swings, head rolls, ankle rotations, and leg and arm shakes.

Breathe. Throughout your warm-up and your test, be sure you are breathing regularly and properly.

Take air in through your nose, and send it down to fill your abdomen.

Exhale through your mouth to empty lungs and deflate the abdomen.

Especially when you are concentrating and focusing, be sure to breathe in a regular rhythm.

Horse warm-up. Just before the test, warm-up your horse.

Start out at a lazy walk on long reins so your horse can blow and stretch his back and neck and relax.

After a few minutes, sit deep, flex your abdominals, put your lower legs on your horse's sides, and gather up the reins.

For about ten minutes, walk or trot your horse along the arena rail, or make large figures such as 60-foot circles or large serpentines.

Let your horse have a little rest break on a long but not loose rein, as you walk for a minute or two.

Pick your horse back up and practice one or two of the transitions or a lateral or collection exercise from this guide.

Good luck! Ride the test well!

Figure 8

- Begin at the center of the arena with your horse facing one of the long sides of the arena.
- Look straight ahead and ride straight forward at a posting trot.
- After 1–2 strides, begin circling your horse to the right.
- Make a large circle to the right that is uniformly round by keeping your aids consistent.
- When approaching the close of the circle, prepare to change your aids to straight.
- Ride straight ahead 1–4 strides, depending on the size of the circle. At the middle of the straight line, change posting.
- Change the bend from straight to left.
- Begin circling your horse to the left at a posting trot.
- Make a large circle to the left that is uniformly round.
- When approaching the close of the second circle, prepare to track straight ahead. Sit the trot for one stride.
- Walk ahead 1–2 strides.
- Halt.

Test Ride Tips

★ The line between the two circles should be parallel to the short ends of the arena. It should not be a diagonal line that makes an X in the middle of the pattern. An X configuration is a lazy way to change direction in a figure 8 and "eats up" part of each circle. The flat line in the center is more correct and more difficult because it requires you to keep your horse in balance.

★ Your ultimate goal is to ride only one stride straight in the center.

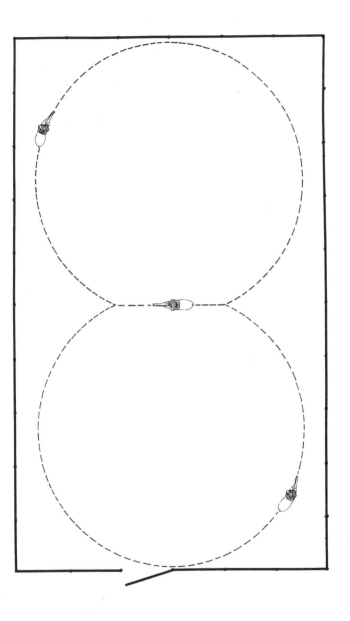

★ Focus on a fence post or cone to keep you straight.
★ During the change of bend from right to left, be ready to catch the hindquarters with your right leg if they try to swing out of the new circle.

To the Examiner...

You are performing an important role for the rider you are observing. Please study the test pattern carefully and know the exact instructions. Always strive to encourage, not discourage, a rider by your comments. Look for details that can help a rider improve. Try to determine whether it is the rider that needs help or if it is the horse that needs work.

The Numbers. *High scores:* There are so many things that can be improved in a horse or rider. If you give high scores right away, there is less room for improvement. *Low scores:* When you must give a very low score, offer at least one positive comment along with your suggestions for improvement.

Each maneuver is scored on a basis of 0–10:

- 10 = excellent, perfect, took my breath away!
- 9 = everything was correct but lacked exquisite smoothness and brilliance
- 8 = good job, everything required was performed but overall it lacked finesse
- 7 = average job, performed correctly but lacked absolute smoothness, promptness, accuracy, evenness
- 6 = minor mistake such as horse bent incorrectly for a few strides or late transition
- 5 = one major mistake such as breaking gait for a few strides but then corrected, wrong lead for a few strides but then corrected
- 4 = two major mistakes made that were corrected
- 3 = three major mistakes made that were corrected
- 2 = one major mistake that wasn't corrected
- 1 = maneuver did not resemble test requirements
- 0 = didn't perform the maneuver

Comments. Be descriptive and creative with your comments — they will help the rider more than numbers because your words will stay in her mind. If you write "poor trot," it doesn't tell much, whereas "a stumble, quick rhythm at beginning of circle, hollow back and short stride" tells the rider much more.

Score Sheet: Beginning English

MOVEMENT	SCORE	COMMENTS
Begin at square halt		
Ride straight at posting trot 1–2 strides		
Ride large circle to right		
Ride straight, change posting		
Change to left bend, begin circle to left		
Ride large circle to left		
Finish circle, track straight		
Sitting trot one stride		
Walk 1–2 strides		
Halt		

TOTAL

90–100	It's time to move on to Intermediate English.
80–89	Work more on the areas your examiner identified, then retest in about a week.
70–79	Plan to spend several weeks improving bending, steadiness, and straightness.
60–69	Ask for specific help from your instructor to improve balance, precision, and control.
50–59	Review all of the exercises in this guide.
0–49	Are you working regularly with an instructor? Is your horse adequately trained?

Other Storey Titles You Will Enjoy

Arena Pocket Guides, by Cherry Hill. Covering both Western and English riding, this six-book series provides illustrated arena exercises and advice for beginners, intermediates, and advanced riders. 32 pages each. Paperback. *Beginning Western Exercises* ISBN 1-58017-045-5, *Intermediate Western Exercises* ISBN 1-58017-046-3, *Advanced Western Exercises* ISBN 1-58017-047-1, *Beginning English Exercises* ISBN 1-58017-044-7, *Intermediate English Exercises* ISBN 1-58017-042-0, *Advanced English Exercises* ISBN 1-58017-043-9.

The Basics of Western Riding, by Charlene Strickland. Covers the Western horse and horse handling, the Western saddle seat, Western tack, becoming a horseman, and trail riding. 160 pages. Paperback. ISBN 1-58017-030-7.

Becoming an Effective Rider, by Cherry Hill. A range of techniques to help any rider reach full potential, whether in recreational riding or formal dressage. 192 pages. Paperback. ISBN 0-88266-688-6.

Competing in Western Shows & Events, by Charlene Strickland. Describes Western horse show basics, the show rules and players, showing intermediate riders, showing working horses, timed events, and arena contests. 144 pages. Paperback. ISBN 1-58017-031-5.

Horse Health Care: A Step-by-Step Photographic Guide, by Cherry Hill. Includes more than 300 close-up photographs and exact instructions explaining bandaging, giving shots, examining teeth, deworming, preventive care, and many other horsekeeping skills. 160 pages. Paperback. ISBN 0-88266-955-9.

Horse Handling & Grooming: A Step-by-Step Photographic Guide, by Cherry Hill. Contains hundreds of close-up photographs for feeding, haltering, tying, grooming, braiding, and blanketing. 160 pages. Paperback. ISBN 0-88266-956-7.

Horsekeeping on a Small Acreage, by Cherry Hill. Focuses on the essentials for designing safe and functional facilities on small areas of land. 196 pages. Paperback. ISBN 0-88266-596-0.

Safe Horse, Safe Rider: A Young Rider's Guide to Responsible Horsekeeping, by Jessie Haas. Beginning with understanding the horse and ending with competitions, includes chapters on horse body language, pastures, catching, and grooming. 160 pages. Paperback. ISBN 0-88266-700-9.

These and other books from Storey Publishing are available wherever quality books are sold or by calling 1-800-441-5700. Visit us at www.storey.com.